FRIENDS
OF ACPL

3 1833 05547 8538

ALLEN COUNTY PUBLIC LIBRARY

W9-CZX-136

Oviraptor

By Joanne Mattern
Illustrations by Jeffrey Mangiat

Reading Consultant: Susan Nations, M.Ed.,
author/literacy coach/consultant in literacy development
Science Consultant: Darla Zelenitsky, Ph.D.,
Assistant Professor of Dinosaur Paleontology at the University of Calgary, Canada

WEEKLY READER®
PUBLISHING

Please visit our web site at www.garethstevens.com.
For a free color catalog describing our list of high-quality books,
call 1-800-542-2595 (USA) or 1-800-387-3178 (Canada).
Our fax: 1-877-542-2596

Library of Congress Cataloging-in-Publication Data

Mattern, Joanne, 1963–
    Oviraptor / by Joanne Mattern ; illustrations by Jeffrey Mangiat.
        p. cm. — (Let's read about dinosaurs)
    Includes bibliographical references and index.
    ISBN-10: 0-8368-9417-0   ISBN-13: 978-0-8368-9417-2 (lib. bdg.)
    ISBN-10: 0-8368-9421-9   ISBN-13: 978-0-8368-9421-9 (softcover)
    1. Oviraptor—Juvenile literature. I. Mangiat, Jeffrey, ill. II. Title.
    QE862.S3M332255   2009
    567.912—dc22   2008025011

This edition first published in 2009 by
Weekly Reader® Books
An Imprint of Gareth Stevens Publishing
1 Reader's Digest Road
Pleasantville, NY 10570-7000 USA

Copyright © 2009 by Gareth Stevens, Inc.

Executive Managing Editor: Lisa M. Herrington
Creative Director: Lisa Donovan
Senior Editor: Barbara Bakowski
Art Director: Ken Crossland
Publisher: Keith Garton

All rights reserved. No part of this book may be reproduced, stored in a retrieval system,
or transmitted in any form or by any means, electronic, mechanical, photocopying,
recording, or otherwise, without the prior written permission of the copyright holder.
For permission, contact **permissions@gspub.com**.

Printed in the United States of America

1 2 3 4 5 6 7 8 9 10 09 08

Table of Contents

Boldface words appear in the glossary.

Small and Speedy

Meet a small dinosaur named Oviraptor (oh-vee-RAP-tor). It lived about 80 million years ago.

Oviraptor looked like a large bird. It weighed about as much as a nine-year-old boy.

Oviraptor had long legs.
It could run very fast.
A long tail helped the
dinosaur **balance**.

tail

Eat or Be Eaten!

Oviraptor was probably an **omnivore** (AHM-nee-vor). It may have eaten meat, plants, eggs, and clams.

Oviraptor had no teeth. It crushed food with its **beak** and strong jaws.

beak

Each arm had three clawed fingers. Oviraptor fought off **predators** with its long claws.

claws

15

Egg Stealer or Egg Sitter?

This dinosaur's name means "egg stealer." Scientists found an Oviraptor **fossil** on top of some eggs. They thought the dinosaur was stealing the eggs to eat them.

fossil

Later, scientists had a new idea. Oviraptor was caring for its own eggs! It sat on a nest, just as birds do.

eggs

19

Scientists have found Oviraptor fossils and eggs in Asia. Fossils help us learn about this special dinosaur.

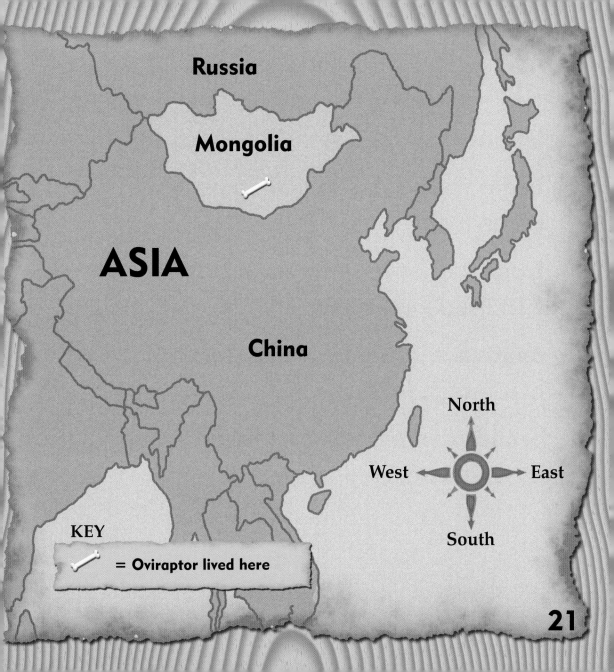

Russia

Mongolia

ASIA

China

North

West — East

South

KEY

= Oviraptor lived here

Glossary

balance: to keep steady and not fall

beak: the hard, sharp mouthpart of an animal

fossil: bones or remains of animals that lived long ago

omnivore: an animal that eats both meat and plants

predators: animals that hunt and eat other animals

For More Information

Books

Dinosaur Babies. I Love Reading: Dino World! (series). Leonie Bennett (Bearport Publishing, 2007)

Oviraptor. Michael P. Goecke (Buddy Books, 2007)

Web Sites

Dinosaurs for Kids: Oviraptor
www.kidsdinos.com/dinosaurs-for-children .php?dinosaur=Oviraptor
Find fun facts, illustrations, a map, and a time line.

Zoom Dinosaurs: Oviraptor
www.enchantedlearning.com/subjects/dinosaurs/ dinos/Oviraptor
Learn more about Oviraptor and where it lived.

Publisher's note to educators and parents: Our editors have carefully reviewed these web sites to ensure that they are suitable for children. Many web sites change frequently, however, and we cannot guarantee that a site's future contents will continue to meet our high standards of quality and educational value. Be advised that children should be closely supervised whenever they access the Internet.

Index

About the Author

Joanne Mattern has written more than 250 books for children. She has written about weird animals, sports, world cities, dinosaurs, and many other subjects. Joanne also works in her local library. She lives in New York state with her husband, four children, and assorted pets. She enjoys animals, music, reading, hiking, and visiting schools to talk about her books.